THE ESSENTIAL KANT

THE ESSENTIAL KANT

Paul Strathern

Typeset by TW Typesetting, Plymouth, Devon
Printed and bound in Great Britain by
Mags Ltd St Ives PLC.

This edition published in Great Britain in 2002 by
Virgin Books Ltd
Thames Wharf Studios
Rainville Road
London
W6 9HA

First published in the USA in 1996 as *Kant in 90 Minutes* by Ivan R Dee

A catalogue record for this book is available from the British Library.

ISBN 0 7535 0674 2

CONTENTS

CONTENTS

THE ESSENTIAL KANT

INTRODUCTION

Just because a thing is impossible, this doesn't mean someone won't try to do it. Kant not only tried but succeeded in achieving the impossible. After Hume had destroyed philosophy and any possibility of constructing a metaphysical system, Kant created the greatest metaphysical system of them all. His motive was to refute Hume, but fortunately he had read only Hume's *Inquiry into Human Understanding*, not the more penetrating scepticism of his earlier *Treatise of Human Nature*. Had Kant read this, he might have produced no system. This would have been a great pity and would have left an entire generation of nineteenth-century German philosophy professors without jobs.

Kant's system is like Newton's idea of gravity. It's not the final answer, but it's close to how we still see the world. You won't go far wrong if you look at the world Kant's way. Hume's philosophy is essentially simplistic: it reduces our philosophical condition to the barren rock of solipsism. Kant, building on the deceptive sands of error, created a wonderful sandcastle of such ingenuity and complexity that it can keep you happily absorbed with your bucket and spade for your entire vacation.

It's difficult to know what to say about Kant's life. He didn't really have one (outside his head). Nothing of any real interest happened to him. But the description of a life of utter tedium need not be boring in itself.

KANT'S LIFE AND WORKS

Immanuel Kant was born on 22 April 1724, in the Baltic city of Königsberg, then the capital of the isolated German province of East Prussia (now Kaliningrad in Russia). Kant's ancestors had emigrated from Scotland in the preceding century and may well have been related to the notorious seventeenth-century Scottish preacher Andrew Cant, who is said to have been the origin of the verb 'to cant' with regard to the use of jargon – a family trait which was to reappear with a vengeance in the philosopher.

At the time of Kant's birth East Prussia was recovering from the devastation of war and plague, which had reduced the population by over half. Kant grew up in an atmosphere of pious poverty. He was the fourth child of the family, which eventually included five sisters and one other brother. Kant's Scottish father was a cutter of leather straps who jocularly claimed that he 'could never make both ends meet' either at home or at work. Kant always remained respectful of his likeable but financially harassed father, and as a child is said to have enjoyed watching him deftly cutting up pieces of leather for harnesses. Yet according to the philosophical psychologist Ben-Ami Scharfstein, in the light of his father's dexterity 'Kant's great clumsiness with his hands is therefore noteworthy'.

Whether or not this is the case, and what precisely it might be noteworthy of, the main early influence in Kant's life was undoubtedly his mother. Frau Kant was a wholly uneducated German woman who is said to have possessed great 'natural intelligence'. It was this which particularly influenced her son Immanuel – or Manelchen as she called him ('Little Manny'). Kant's mother would take him for walks in the countryside and tell him the names of the plants and flowers. At night she would show him the stars, naming them and their constellations. She was a pious woman, and her loving but austere ways also helped shape her son's moral character. This dual insistence on facts and moral obligation was to remain with Kant throughout his life and played a leading role in his philosophy. Kant's most celebrated remark, made over fifty years later, harks directly back to these early days with his mother: 'The starry heavens above and the moral law within fill the mind with an ever new and increasing admiration and awe, the more often and the more steadily we reflect.'

Kant was brought up in a strict Pietist atmosphere and from age eight until sixteen went to the local Pietist school. Here his exceptional intelligence and keen thirst for learning quickly grew irked with the endless religious instruction. This dislike of formal religion was to remain with him for the rest of his days (in mature life he never attended church). Despite this, Kant retained much of the Pietist outlook, with its belief in a simple way of life and adherence to strict morality.

In 1737 Kant's mother died and received a pauper's burial. Kant was thirteen at the time and has indicated that he experienced his first sexual stirrings around this period. Psychologists have suggested that the loss of his beloved mother at this stage of puberty caused him to feel guilty and repress his sexual feelings. Either this or they simply withered away. Whatever the cause, from now on Kant was to live a life of sexual repression which assumed heroic proportions.

At the age of seventeen Kant was admitted to the University of Königsberg as a theological student. Initially he was given financial assistance by the local Pietist church, but he also helped support himself by tutoring some of his more backward colleagues. He soon grew bored with theology and began showing a strong interest in mathematics and physics. He read Newton, who opened his eyes to science and the great advances being made in all parts of it, from astronomy to zoology. Science based on experiment could only be accommodated in an empiricist philosophy, that is, one which bases our knowledge of the world on experience. In 1746, when Kant was twenty-two, his father died. Kant and his five younger sisters were left penniless. The younger of these sisters were taken in by a Pietist family while the older ones went to work as chambermaids. Kant applied unsuccessfully for a job at a local school and was forced to leave the university without taking a degree.

For the next nine years Kant supported himself as a tutor to wealthy families in the surrounding countryside. For a while he was employed by the Count and Countess Keyserling (the aristocratic family which was later to produce the pseudophilosopher Hermann Keyserling, whose uplifting but bogus ideas were to prove such a comfort to disillusioned society matrons after

World War I). Whenever Kant had a little extra cash he would send some of it to his less fortunate sisters, a habit he continued throughout his later life. His five sisters were to continue living in Königsberg (a city with just fifty thousand inhabitants) throughout the whole of Kant's life. Yet he saw none of them for over twenty-five years. When one of his sisters finally came to visit him he did not even recognise her. After it was explained to him who she was, he apologised to the rest of the company for her lack of culture. Kant may not have been a social snob, but he was renowned for his inability to tolerate fools. Even in his own family, it would seem.

Yet this incident raises a curious point. Kant's sister must surely have borne more than a passing resemblance to their mother, both intellectually and physically. She would even have been around the same age as Kant's mother when she brought him up. Does this mean that Kant's celebrated love for his mother had become so deep that he no longer recognised it? Suggestion has been made that Kant unconsciously resented the repressive nexus – facts, morality, sexual extinction – imposed on him by his mother. His inability to recognise his sister (or indeed have anything to do with her) may well have followed from this, but we have no way of knowing. (Kant's sheer lack of life has perversely attracted far more attention from psychologists than the *comparatively* normal life lived by other philosophers.)

Kant may have been indifferent towards his own family, but he appears to have enjoyed life among the rich families where he was employed as a tutor. His appearance was as much an oddity as his character. He was less than five feet tall, and his head was disproportionately large for his body. His frame suffered from a slight corkscrew twist, which made his left shoulder droop, his right shoulder curve back, and his head tend to lean to one side. Dressed in threadbare clothes and with scarcely a pfennig to his name, he had not exactly been the hit of the campus at the University of Königsberg (which was itself hardly a centre of cosmopolitan society). But now, decked out by his employers in his elegant tutor's outfit, and encouraged to mingle with family guests, Kant positively blossomed. He soon developed a ready wit, acquired a veneer of sophisticated assurance, and became a mean hand at the card and billiard tables. When the families departed for their summer vacations in the country, Kant accompanied them, sometimes journeying almost forty miles from Königsberg. (This was the farthest he was ever to travel from his provincial home throughout his life.) But this period of *comparative* elegance was only a phase.

In 1755, at the age of thirty-one, Kant was at last able to take his degree at the University of Königsberg, partly owing to the charity of a Pietist benefactor. This was late to be finishing a degree; and, as we shall see, Kant was an unusually late developer. By this age almost all the other major philosophers had already begun formulating the ideas for which they would be remembered. Not until two decades later did Kant really begin to produce original philosophy.

Kant was now able to take up a post at the university as a *privatdozent* (junior lecturer). This post he held for the next fifteen years, living a bachelor academic existence of unremitting industry. During this time he lectured mainly on mathematics and physics, and published treatises on a wide range of scientific subjects. These included volcanoes, the nature of winds, anthropology, the cause of earthquakes, fire, the ageing of the earth, even the planets (which he predicted would all one day be inhabited, those farthest from the sun developing the species with the highest intelligence).

Yet Kant's natural bent was towards speculation. He continued to read widely in philosophy. In rationalistic philosophy his ideas were most influenced by Newton and Leibniz. Newton's greatest achievements may have been in physics and mathematics, but in those days these subjects were still considered part of philosophy, as 'natural philosophy'. The full title of Newton's greatest work is *Philosophiae Naturalis Principia Mathematica* (*The Mathematical Principles of Natural Philosophy*). Kant studied Newton with sufficient thoroughness to propose a 'New Theory of Motion and Rest' which opposed Newton's view. The fact that he had misunderstood Newton is not the point. He was being led to speculate on systems which encompassed the universe and was willing to question the greatest intellect of the era on his own ground.

According to Leibniz the physical world of cause and effect proved the inner harmony of the world's moral purpose. Reading Leibniz led Kant to see humanity as not only participating in nature, but over and above this participating in the ultimate purpose of the universe.

At the same time Kant's interest in the philosophy of science led him to read the Scottish philosopher Hume. Kant was impressed by Hume's insistence on experience as the basis of all knowledge. This squared with the scientific approach. But Kant found himself unable to accept the sceptical conclusions that Hume drew from his rigid empiricism. According to Hume, all we experience is a sequence of perceptions – and this means that such notions as cause and effect, bodies and things, even the controlling hand of God the creator, are all mere suppositions or beliefs. None of them is ever actually experienced.

Surprisingly Kant was also struck by the emotional appeal of Rousseau. The first of the romantics, Rousseau was the most unacademic of all philosophers, believing in personal expression through emotion more than rational thought. His advocacy of liberty was to prove a heady inspiration for the French Revolution. Kant may have been an essentially dry character, but there was something in Rousseau that touched a chord in his deeply suppressed emotions. Beneath the façade of the prim academic beat the heart of a closet romantic – and this was later to become apparent in his philosophy. But for the time being all these disparate elements – Newton, Leibniz, Hume, Rousseau – remained just that. Not until Kant found a way of reconciling and absorbing these influences would he be able to produce original philosophy. And the enormity of such a task would take a long time.

Perhaps Kant became impatient for there now occurred an odd episode. Instead of publishing another serious academic work, Kant wrote a curious satirical book called *Dreams of a Ghost-Seer Elucidated by Means of Metaphysical Dreams*. The 'ghost-seer' of the title is the Swedish visionary mystic Swedenborg, famous for his descriptions of his lengthy travels through heaven and hell. In 1756 Swedenborg had published his eight-volume masterwork *Arcana coelestia* (*The Secrets of Heaven*). Unfortunately sales did not go well, and after ten years only four copies had been sold. One of these is now known to have been bought by Kant. These volumes of metaphysical mumbo jumbo had a profound effect on Kant – enough to inspire him to write an entire book satirising them. As Kant whimsically declares in his introduction: 'The author confesses with a certain humility that he was so simple-minded as to track down the truth of some tales of the sort mentioned. He found – as usual, where one has nothing to look for – he found nothing.' Yet it soon becomes evident that Kant's mockery of 'the worst visionary of them all' and of 'sundry airy thought-worlds ... hewn ... out of fraudulent concepts' is not quite what it seems. Beneath his consistent raillery and expressions of intellectual contempt is an unmistakable element of profoundly serious interest in Swedenborg. Kant longed to believe in metaphysics (even if not in quite such an extreme form), but his formidable intellectual development was beginning to close down this avenue.

Kant's writing style is notoriously prolix and difficult, but by all accounts his lectures were quite the opposite. His body was so short and twisted that only his bewigged head, with its prim, precise features, was visible above the lectern. But this talking head was a font of wit, fascinating erudition and ideas. Kant's lectures were a great hit, and his fame soon spread, encouraged by his stream of treatises on scientific subjects. His celebrated summer lectures on geography always attracted crowds from outside the university. These continued for over thirty years and established Kant as the first academic teacher of physical geography, despite the fact that throughout his life he never set eyes on a mountain and may never even have seen the open sea (which was almost twenty miles away). Kant's vivid and perceptive descriptions brought to life the wonders of the distant lands that he read about with such enthusiasm during the long winter evenings, when the freezing Baltic fog drifted in through the streets of remote provincial Königsberg.

Kant now also began delivering lectures on philosophy, and here it soon became apparent that he had journeyed far and wide through the hostile territories of ethics and epistemology, beyond the ultima Thule of logic and even into regions so remote from civilisation as metaphysics (and had lived to tell the tale). Meanwhile treatises on more amenable subjects, such as fireworks, military defence, and the theory of the heavens, continued to pour from his pen. Despite this, Kant was twice refused a professorship at the University of Königsberg. The reasons for this are unclear, but one suspects an element of provincial snobbery. Or perhaps they just didn't like him. Either way, Kant certainly liked Königsberg. When he was offered the prestigious post of professor of poetry at the University of Berlin, he turned it down.

Fortunately in 1770 the Königsberg University authorities relented, and Kant was appointed professor of logic and metaphysics. Now, aged forty-six, he had grown increasingly critical of Leibniz and his rationalistic disciples who had become the dominant force in

German philosophy. Hume's empiricism seemed undeniable, and reluctantly Kant even became convinced by Hume's scepticism. Objects, cause and effect, continuity, even the self – all these appeared to be fallacious notions. They remained beyond the reach of our experience, which was the only certain source of our knowledge. Kant accepted this because it seemed to him intellectually irrefutable. But he was not happy with this barren state of affairs. There appeared to be no further room for philosophy to continue. Was this really the end?

Then one day, while studying Hume's *Inquiry Concerning Human Understanding*, Kant 'awoke from his dogmatic slumbers'. In a flash of inspiration he saw how he could construct a system and answer the destructive scepticism of Hume which had threatened to destroy metaphysics forever.

For eleven years Kant published nothing, but continued working out his philosophy. Already he had begun living a life of extreme regularity, and during this period his routine began to achieve legendary status. In the words of Heine: 'Rising, coffee drinking, writing, lecturing, dining, walking, each had its set time. And when Immanuel Kant, in his grey coat, cane in hand, appeared at the door of his house, and strolled towards the small avenue of linden trees which is still called "The Philosopher's Walk", the neighbours knew that it was exactly half past three by the clock. So he promenaded up and down, during all seasons: and when the weather was gloomy, or the grey clouds threatened rain, his old servant Lampe was to be seen plodding anxiously after, with a large umbrella under his arm, like a symbol of Prudence.' Only on one famous occasion is Kant said to have broken this routine: on the day he started reading Rousseau's *Émile*, when he became so absorbed that he missed his walk in order to finish it. Only Rousseau's avowal of romantic emotion could make him forget his routine. But such feelings were not enough to cause any serious break with the habits of a lifetime. Although Kant twice considered marriage during these years, on both occasions he took so long making up his mind that by the time he'd decided (in favour, on both occasions), one of the ladies had married someone else, and the other had moved to another city. Kant was not a man to be rushed into decisions. Yet his admiration for Rousseau's romantic ideas was not confined to theory. Years later, when many of Rousseau's ideas came to fruition with the outbreak of the French Revolution, Kant wept with joy, a rare sentiment in the fiercely conservative provincial Prussian city of Königsberg, and probably unique among its university establishment.

In 1781 Kant at last published his *Critique of Pure Reason*, generally regarded as his masterpiece. Yet not all his readers were enthusiastic. When Kant sent a copy of the manuscript to his friend Herz, it was eventually returned only half read. Herz claimed that to continue reading Kant's work any further would have been to court insanity. And you may well feel the same. In his *Critique of Pure Reason* Kant decided to dispense with many interesting arguments and concrete examples, for fear of making his work too long. Even so, in the translated version it runs to over eight hundred pages. And most of it is like this: 'The apodictical proposition cogitates the assertorical as determined by these very laws of the understanding, consequently affirming as a priori, and in this manner it expresses . . .' Even in the finest translation it only *sounds* better: 'La proposizione apodittica concepisce il guidizio assertorio determinato secondo queste legge dell'intelletto stresso e, per consequenza, come affirmativo a priori; ed esprime cosi . . .' You just don't want to know what it's like in German (the miracle is that Herz managed to get as far as halfway before fearing for his sanity).

But don't let this distract you from the magnificence of Kant's actual system. Kant's aim was to restore metaphysics. He agreed with Hume and the empiricists that there are no such things as innate ideas; but he denied that all knowledge was derived from experience. The empiricists argued that all knowledge must conform to experience; Kant brilliantly reversed this by saying that all experience must conform to knowledge. According to Kant, space and time are subjective. They are our way of perceiving the world. In a way they are like irremovable spectacles, without which we are incapable of making sense of our experience. But these are not the only subjective elements that help us understand our experience. Kant explained that there are various 'categories' (as he called them) which we conceive of by means of our understanding working independently of experience. These categories include such things as quality, quantity and relation. These too are like irremovable spectacles. We cannot see the world in any other way than in terms of quality, quantity and so forth. But through these irremovable spectacles we can see only the phenomena of the world – we can never perceive the actual noumena, the true reality that supports or gives rise to these phenomena.

It has been observed that only a man who has never seen a mountain could possibly believe that space is not there outside us, only part of our perceptual apparatus. And common sense would seem to agree with this. But such gauche ad hominem objections have nothing to do with philosophy.

Space and time, and the categories (which include such notions as plurality, causality and existence), can only be applied to the phenomena of our experience. If we apply them to things which are not experienced, we end up with 'antinomies' – that is, contrasting statements, both of which can apparently be proved by purely intellectual argument. In this way Kant demolishes all purely intellectual arguments for the existence (or nonexistence) of God. We simply cannot apply such a category as existence to such a nonempirical entity.

As we can see, Kant was not in favour of a wholesale return to metaphysics in his *Critique of Pure Reason*. By 'pure reason' Kant here means a priori reason – something that can be known *prior* to experience. Hume had denied such transcendental entities (ones that 'transcend' experience). But Kant was convinced that he had restored this transcendental/metaphysical element to philosophy in the form of his 'categories of pure reason'. Hume's sceptical view may seem simplistic, and is certainly unworkable if we wish to live in the real world. (His denial of causality effectively reduces the whole of science to the status of metaphysics.) Kant's view, on the other hand, is immensely subtle and sophisticated – but it scarcely overcomes Hume's point from a *philosophical* point of view. We may not be able to experience the world without conceiving of space, quantity and so forth. But it is difficult to argue that these are not an integral *part* of that experience, or to see how they could exist without it (that is, prior to it).

On the other hand, Kant's argument that we can never know the real world carries considerable weight. All the things we perceive are only phenomena. The thing-in-itself (the noumena) which supports or gives rise to these phenomena remains forever unknowable. And there is no reason why it should resemble *in any way* our perceptions. The phenomena are perceived by way of *our* categories, which have nothing whatsoever to do with the thing-in-itself. This remains beyond quality, quantity, relation and the like.

After publishing the *Critique*, Kant continued to live his life of rigid routine. This did not preclude an element of socialising, though this was always very much a minor element in his life. He maintained relations with a number of his brighter students as well as a few members of the faculty. Yet he was never close with any of them. (No one was addressed with the informal *du*, even after decades of social contact.) Thought was his life. 'For a scholar, thinking is a means of nourishment, without which, when he is *awake* or *alone*, he cannot live.' He was more intent on knowing himself than anyone else. But the task of getting to know Kant proved as difficult for himself as it was for others. 'I do not understand myself sufficiently,' he complained. Perhaps he was afraid of what he might find. Here Scharfstein makes a fundamental point: '*This* thing-in-itself was not simply unknown, it was forbidden; for it was Kant's suppressed emotional life, I take it, and he was afraid that if it was revealed, he would be devastated.'

Kant was well aware that he had no friends. But this didn't bother him. He was fond of quoting Aristotle's remark: 'My friends, I have no friends.' Indeed, he positively recommended this state. 'Friendship is a restriction of favourable sentiments to a single subject, and is very pleasant to him towards whom they are directed, but also a proof that generality and goodwill are lacking.'

Psychologists have claimed that Kant's inability (or unwillingness) to form close relationships indicated a profound unhappiness. But Kant does not appear to have been unhappy. Quite the opposite. Those who met him remarked on his cheerfulness. 'Kant's disposition was by nature meant for cheerfulness. He saw the world with a glad look . . . and transferred his cheerfulness to external things. Therefore he was usually disposed to be happy,' was a typical observation by one of his colleagues.

Seven years after the publication of his *Critique of Pure Reason*, Kant published his *Critique of Practical Reason*. Shorter than its predecessor, it makes no other concessions to the reader. (When I came across the first edition owned by Coleridge – an ardent fan of Kant – I couldn't help noticing that some of the pages were still uncut.)

In this work Kant reinstated God, who was no longer deemed unspeakable because he didn't fit into the categories. The *Critique of Practical Reason* is devoted to the ethical part of Kant's system. Here, instead of seeking metaphysical grounds for our perception, he seeks them for our morality. Kant was searching for nothing less than the fundamental moral law. But surely it was impossible to discover such a law that would please everyone? From Christians to Buddhists, from liberals to Prussians – all believing in the same fundamental good? Kant believed it was possible to discover a basic law; but he did so by sidestepping what most would consider to be the main question. Good and evil were not his concern here. He was not seeking to discover some essence of all the different interpretations of these basic moral concepts. Kant stressed that he was seeking the *grounds* of morality rather than its content. As with pure reason, so with practical reason: what was needed was a set of a priori principles like the categories.

In fact, Kant eventually came up with only one principle: his 'categorical imperative'. This was the a priori ground for all moral action: its metaphysical premise. In an analogous way to the categories of pure reason, this gives a framework to our ethical thinking (practical reason) though without giving it any specific moral content. Kant's categorical imperative states: 'Act only in accord with a principle which you would at the same time will to be a universal law.'

This principle led Kant to believe that we should act in accordance with our duty, not according to our feelings, and resulted in some odd conclusions. For instance, Kant stated that the moral worth of an action should not be judged according to its consequences but only in so far as it was done for the sake of duty. This is plainly daft – if morality is to do with society, rather than just individual self-righteousness.

Kant intended his categorical imperative as a mere framework, empty of moral content. But it isn't quite. It still contains traces of moral content. The morality of conformity, for a start. Kant's categorical imperative implies that everyone should act in precisely the same way, regardless of temperament or task. Should the head of a government act with the same moral scruples as the head of a monastery? Should he even try? Should Churchill have tried to behave like Ghandi? Or vice versa? Perhaps all systems are bound to lead to such rigidities. (But without any ethical system we would be completely lost – unable to make any value judgements whatsoever.)

Kant's ethical system also led him to believe that we should never tell a lie, regardless of what consequences this might involve. He was well aware of the implications of this argument, but he stuck to it nonetheless. 'To tell a falsehood to a murderer, who is in pursuit of a friend of yours who has taken refuge in your house, would be a crime.'

Are we to believe that Kant would have delivered a Jewish friend to Nazis? No: everything we know about him suggests that he would have followed the dictates of duty here. His highly active mind would quickly have discovered a duty which forbade him to hand over his friend.

Yet this question of never telling a lie exposes a distinct flaw in Kant's system. For make no mistake about it, Kant took this business about lies *extremely* seriously. He even spent time agonising over the question of whether it was permissible to end a letter with the customary conclusion of the period, 'Your obedient servant'. Was this a lie? Kant insisted he was no man's servant, that he had no intention of obeying his correspondents. But eventually he seems to have relented on this matter.

Yet on more serious literary matters he remained unbending. He was against the reading of novels. They caused our thought to become 'fragmentary' and weakened our memory. 'For it would be ridiculous to memorise novels in order to relate them to others.' (The implication that Kant memorised all other books he read is not to be lightly dismissed.) Here Kant overlooks the fact that reading Rousseau's novel *Heloise* was a formative experience, which he seems to have accomplished without exploding his thought into fragments or softening his memory.

Kant enjoyed reading poetry, but only if it was an intellectual harmonisation of virtue and sentiment. Unrhymed poetry was simply prose gone mad. Music was a different and altogether more difficult matter. Music alone could penetrate the carapace of repression that protected his unexpressed emotions, and in consequence he was particularly harsh on it. He detested folk music (such as his mother had often sung to him). Musicians were characterless because what they played reduced everything to feeling. He recommended that his students avoid listening to music because it would make them effeminate. Yet he couldn't stop attending concerts himself – until the day he attended one in memory of the philosopher Moses Mendelssohn. This struck him as nothing less than endless moaning, and he never attended a concert again.

In 1790, at the age of sixty-six, Kant published the third and final part of his monsterpiece, his *Critique of Judgement*. This is ostensibly concerned with aesthetic judgements but also deals with theology (and much, much more). Kant argues that the existence of art presupposes the artist, and that it is through the beauty of the world that we recognise a benign creator. As he had previously implied, we recognise God's work in the stars of the heavens as well as in our inner inclination to do good.

As with his theory of perception and his ethical theory, Kant sought to establish a metaphysical basis for his theory of aesthetic judgement. He wished to establish an a priori principle that made our apprehension of beauty possible. Here Kant was on rather more shaky ground. It's always difficult to get a consensus on beauty. Some consider the Swiss Alps pure chocolate candy, finding spiritual sustenance in expressionism. Others do not. Such views are seemingly irreconcilable. But Kant was determined to bring *everything* within the bounds of his system.

Kant argues: 'A person who describes something as beautiful insists that everyone *ought* to give the object in question his approval.' The similarity to the categorical imperative is evident, but here it simply doesn't work – except in the personal pejorative sense. Once again we are faced with the conformity syndrome. Just because I find Francis Bacon's picture of a screaming pope beautiful, doesn't mean I expect everyone else to do so.

Kant goes on to argue that it is only through the unity and consistency of nature that science is possible. This unity cannot be proved but must be assumed. Related to this idea is the notion that nature is purposive. Kant claims the purposiveness of nature is 'a special a priori concept'. As we now know, this concept is not necessary to an assumption of the unity and consistency of nature. And even the latter are now questioned by quantum theory.

Kant insisted that although we cannot prove the world has a purpose, we must look upon it 'as if' it has a purpose. Kant didn't deny the evil, ugly and apparently purposeless aspects of the world, but he thought they counted for a lot less than their more uplifting opposites. In the next century Schopenhauer was to take precisely the opposite point of view – with perhaps more justification. In the end, neither the optimistic nor the pessimistic point of view can in any way be endorsed by proof, and remain ultimately a matter of temperament.

Meanwhile Kant continued with his indefatigable routine, and the citizens of Königsberg continued to set their watches according to when Kant began his afternoon walk: 3:00 p.m. *precisely*.

Kant's view that time is all in the mind and has nothing to do with reality may have had something to do with his living in East Prussia. This territory was surrounded to the south and the west by Poland, which lived one hour ahead of East Prussia. And over the eastern border was Russia, which by its Julian calendar was eleven days behind the rest of Europe. The nearest people who kept the same time as East Prussia were two borders away, across Poland to the west, in Germany.

Kant lived on Prinzessinnenstrasse, in a house that was demolished in 1893. Here he was looked after by his grumpy old servant Lampe, with whom he was capable of being equally grumpy. Everything had to be done exactly right. Lampe even had to help his master out of his clothes each night in the correct order. And when Kant went to bed he invariably wore one nightcap in summer and two in winter, which could be very cold indeed in Königsberg when the nearby Baltic froze over.

In the manner of all pernickety domestic tyrants, Kant was always concerned about Lampe's spiritual welfare. Indeed, Kant declared that he had reinstated God in his *Critique of Practical Reason* expressly in order to give Lampe something to believe in. Lampe may not have fully appreciated this: we have no evidence of his gratitude. It's a little easier to guess Lampe's attitude towards his master's unique philosophical method of holding up his stockings – by means of pieces of string which ran up through his trouser pockets and were attached to springs contained in two small boxes. (This last piece of information sounds utterly preposterous but is confirmed by a number of independent sources, one of whom suggests that Kant's father being in the strap-making business had something to do with it.)

Like many possessed of an independent and imaginative mind, Kant was a practising hypochondriac. Indeed, he was so good at it that he was the only person who ever noticed anything wrong with him. Throughout his long life this frail little man with the twisted frame was never known to be ill. His hypochondria involved him in a tireless and systematic regime. One of his habits was to breathe only through his nose, especially when he went on his walk in cold weather. This meant that during autumn, winter and spring he was incapable of replying to anyone who addressed him on the street because he refused to open his mouth in case he might catch a cold.

Kant was fortunate while publishing his three great *Critiques*. During this period the political situation in Prussia was unusually tolerant, not a quality often associated with that country. It is doubtful that Kant would have been able to publish such works in most other European countries. He appreciated this and dedicated the *Critique of Pure Reason* to Zedlitz, Frederick the Great's minister of education. As befits a dry-as-dust provincial professor, Kant was outwardly respectful towards the king. But at heart he was surprisingly revolutionary. And he had nothing but contempt for the French philosophers who hung around Frederick's court.

When Frederick the Great died in 1786 and Frederick William II ascended to the throne, Kant found himself in hot water. Wöllner, an ardent Pietist, became the minister responsible for education and charged Kant with misusing his philosophy to distort the Bible. Someone at the ministry had evidently managed to struggle through the eight hundred pages of the *Critique of Pure Reason* and had discovered that it denied all proofs of the existence of God. Kant was required to pledge that he would not lecture or write further books on a religious subject. He wrote a letter to the king, giving his word that he would obey this order. But when the king died in 1797 Kant considered that he was released from his promise, and returned to the subject with renewed vigour. (As we see here, Kant's views on lying were susceptible to adaptation when the occasion arose.)

By now Kant was approaching seventy. Years of practice had perfected his hypochondria to the point where he was a master of this art. Each month he would send to the Königsberg chief of police for the latest mortality statistics, and from these he would calculate his own life expectancy. He became convinced that constipation clouded his brain, and he added an impressive array of laxatives to his laboratory-sized medicine chest. Avidly he would read through the journals describing the latest medical discoveries to determine whether he had any new diseases. Alarmed colleagues who attempted to dissuade him from this hobby were quickly put in their place. Kant knew far more about illness than any mere professor of medicine at the University of Königsberg. On this topic, as on all others, he could not tolerate contradiction. (Unlike other similarly afflicted egoists, he was invariably right, and he knew it.)

University professors may have been able to tolerate such treatment, but it proved too much for his servant Lampe, who had to put up with it all the time. After decades of faithful service, Lampe eventually took to the bottle and had to be dismissed.

Meanwhile Kant continued stoically resisting the attentions of his family. He continued to justify his lack of contact with his sisters by explaining that they were not up to his intellectual level. (After the death of Newton, it's probable that no one in Europe fulfilled this criterion.) When pressed further he said his sisters were pleasant enough, but he had nothing in common with them because they lacked culture. Yet this excuse was certainly invalid with regard to his brother, who had grown to be a cultured professional man but was equally ignored by Kant. This brother dearly longed for social contact with his famous philosophical sibling and regularly wrote letters to him suggesting that they meet, to no avail. At one stage he pleaded to Kant: 'I can no longer bear that such separation should continue, we are brothers.' Kant often took as long as two years to reply to these letters, claiming he had been too busy to write earlier. At the age of sixty-eight, after a delay of two and a half years in replying to his brother's latest letter begging for a meeting, Kant wrote assuring him that he would bear his brother in his thoughts during the short period of life remaining to him, but he carefully refrained from mentioning any meeting.

As he grew older Kant became increasingly solitary and misanthropic. 'Life is a burden to me,' he confessed at last, 'I am tired of bearing it. And if the angel of death were to come this night and call me from here, I would raise my hand and say, "God be praised!" ' Yet he still continued avidly with his hobby, which was presumably intended to prolong his life. Any thought of putting an end to it all was dismissed. He was not afraid to commit suicide, but it was morally wrong. Increasingly he began suffering from nightmares. Each night in his sleep he would find himself surrounded by footpads, stalked by murderers. The paranoid symptoms are unmistakable. He declared: 'Everyone almost hates the other, tries to raise himself above his fellow men, is full of envy, jealousy and other fiendish vices. Man is not a god, he is a devil.' He concluded that 'if a man were to say and write all he thinks, there would be nothing more horrible on God's earth than man.' These last two quotes are curiously revealing of how he must have viewed himself at the end of a crotchety but largely blameless life. (It wasn't his fault about Lampe, who could always have sought employment elsewhere. And he may not have seen his sisters, but he regularly sent them money.)

Kant's natural cheerfulness was now being swamped by the rising tide of his suppressed emotional life. He was certainly unhappy, but he was determined to remain true to himself to the end. He insisted that he didn't mind being unhappy – an attitude quite consistent with his philosophy. In the *Critique of Practical Reason* he had declared that he found it 'astonishing how intelligent men have thought of declaring happiness as a universal practical law'. In his view, happiness and morality had nothing essential to do with each other. We may be gratified when we perform an act of virtue, but Kant was unable to comprehend 'how a mere thought containing nothing sensuous can produce a sensation of pleasure or displeasure'. Such could only have been the expression of a mind utterly withdrawn from the emotions. (Even the driest of mathematicians acknowledge their pleasure on arriving at a difficult solution.)

Yet Kant did admit to one experience that regularly gave him pleasure. His secret vice was characteristically solitary: he enjoyed watching birds and would wait impatiently for their return each spring. According to a colleague: 'The one joy that nature still allowed him . . . was the return of a warbler that sang outside the window in his garden. Even in his joyless old age, this one joy remained to him. If his friend remained away too long, he said, "It must still be very cold on the Apennines" .' Scharfstein, upon whose brilliantly perceptive sketch of Kant's life I have drawn heavily, suggests that the birds represented freedom for Kant. Yet freedom from what? The tyranny of his own nature, certainly. But also perhaps freedom from thought – that very element which he had allowed to enslave his life, the element with which he sought to imprison the entire world within his system.

For the last decade of his life Kant devoted himself to a mammoth philosophical work which he was never to finish. He intended to call this work *Transition from the Metaphysical Foundations of Natural Science to Physics*. Unlike Kant's earlier works, this is definitively unreadable. Bravely risking insanity, several experts have tried to scale this Everest of the German Metaphysical Himalayas but have returned gasping for air and incapable of coherent communication. As far as we can gather from these survivors, Kant advances his general a priori structure for a science of nature, showing in exhaustive detail how this can be extended to apply to particular sciences. The emphasis here is on the 'exhaustive detail'.

Kant now became a sad figure, his great faculties gradually failing. It is said that hypochondria is often a defence mechanism against paranoia. Yet despite diligent and exhaustive practice at his hobby, Kant's paranoia gradually began to get the upper hand. He started to experience pressure on his brain, which he decided was caused by a rare form of electricity in the air. This same electricity he thought responsible for the cat epidemics which had recently broken out in Copenhagen and Vienna. Such involvement with 'electrical powers' is often associated with schizophrenia.

But Kant was never mad. His illness was merely the tight knots that had held him so closely bound throughout his life beginning to loosen. He was fading fast. The few chosen colleagues and favoured students who were invited to dinner would watch in saddened silence as his mind wandered. Then his new servant would lead him away. On 8 October 1803, Kant was ill for the first time in his life. He had a mild stroke after eating too much of his favourite 'English cheese'. After four months of increasing debilitation he died on 12 February 1804. His last words were '*Es ist gut*' (It is good). He was buried in the cathedral, his tomb inscribed with the statement that inclined him towards the God he certainly believed in but never publicly worshipped – words which harked back to an intense small boy listening to a well-meaning mother whom he certainly worshipped: 'The starry heavens above and the moral law within fill the mind with an ever new and increasing admiration and awe, the more often and the more steadily we reflect.'

A DIALOGUE ON KANT AND METAPHYSICS

QUESTION: What is Kant's *Critique of Pure Reason* about?

ANSWER: Metaphysics.

Q: What exactly is metaphysics?

A: This word began as a mistake and has ended up by being regarded as a mistake. In between times it was the main topic of philosophy.

Q: This still doesn't answer the question. What precisely does metaphysics mean?

A: Nothing at all, according to most modern philosophers.

Q: Well, what did it originally mean?

A: This word was first used to refer to certain philosophical works of Aristotle – the ones in his collected works that came after his great work on physics. They became known as the 'beyond Physics' works, which in Greek was *meta-physics*.

Q: But this still doesn't tell me what it means.

A: In these works 'beyond Physics', Aristotle dealt with 'the science of things transcending what is physical or natural'.

Q: And what does that mean?

A: It is the science that deals with the first theoretical principles over and above the physical world. These are the principles that govern our knowledge of that same physical world. In other words, metaphysics deals with whatever transcends the physical world we experience.

Q: But how do we know there is anything beyond the physical world we experience?

A: We don't. Which is why most modern philosophers dismiss such metaphysics as a mistake.

Q: But Kant didn't?

A: Kant was determined to create a new metaphysics. Before him, Hume had arrived at much the same conclusion as those modern philosophers. Hume thought he had destroyed the possibility of metaphysics.

Q: How?

A: By doubting everything that he couldn't confirm from his own experience. This extreme scepticism ruled out all kinds of things that humanity had believed in through the centuries but had never actually experienced.

Q: Such as?

A: God, for instance.

Q: But what Hume said didn't seem to make much difference. People still went on believing in God.

A: Yes, but it was not increasingly understood that they did this through a leap of faith, rather than as a result of direct experience or rational argument.

Q: So Hume's 'disproof' of metaphysics didn't make any difference at all?

A: In fact, it made a huge difference. Especially to scientists and philosophers.

Q: How?

A: In ruling out everything except what we can verify through experience, Hume ruled out a lot more than

God. More important for the scientists and philosophers, he ruled out causality.

Q: How?

A: According to Hume, all we know from experience is that one thing follows another. We can never know that one thing *causes* another. We cannot go *beyond* our experience and say that. We never actually *experience* one thing causing another, only one thing following another.

Q: So?

A: This strikes at the heart of all our scientific knowledge. According to Hume, science based on causality is metaphysical, not empirical. It can never be verified. And verification is the very basis of our knowledge. Likewise philosophy. According to Hume, we can never prove the statements of philosophy, unless they are a result of direct experience.

Q: Such as?

A: Such as the statement, 'This apple is green'.

Q: But that means philosophy can say practically nothing.

A: Precisely. And this is the extreme difficulty that Kant tried to overcome in his philosophy.

Q: How?

A: He tried to show that despite Hume's devastating scepticism, it was still possible to build a metaphysics. This would be the basis for a universal and logically necessary form of knowledge – one that would remain impervious to Hume's scepticism. Kant first set this down in his *Critique of Pure Reason*.

Q: So Kant's metaphysics was an attempt at some kind of ultimate science which guarantees the truth of our knowledge?

A: Precisely.

Q: And how did he set about this?

A: Kant put forward what he called his 'critical philosophy'. This undertook a profound analysis of epistemology – a study of the very basis on which our knowledge rests. According to Kant, we make certain judgements that are indispensable to all knowledge. These judgements he classified as 'synthetic a priori'. By synthetic he meant they were not analytic, and the knowledge they contained was not implied in the original concept. For instance, 'The ball is round' is an analytic statement because the concept 'roundness' is contained within the concept 'ball'. But 'The ball is shiny' is a synthetic judgement. It says something more about the ball than is contained in the original concept, in the same way as an empirical statement. By a priori, Kant meant judgements that are necessary and universal. They had to be true prior to any experience, and are made by the use of reason alone. Unlike judgements made as a result of experience, they are not particular and contingent. That is, they don't just apply to one instance and have no logical necessity – such as statements like 'This horse has won the Derby' and 'That horse is brown'.

Like any scientific judgement, these synthetic a priori statements must be undeniable and universally true. In other words, they must have the same force and strength as an analytic statement, though they are synthetic. And they must be applicable to experience while remaining prior to it.

Kant's basic question was, 'How are synthetic a priori statements possible?' He now applied this question to mathematics, physics and metaphysics. According to Kant, mathematics deals with space and time. Kant argued that, contrary to appearances, space and time are in fact a priori – that is, they are not part of our experience but a necessary prior condition of that experience. We could have no experience without these 'forms of our sensibility'.

Kant then goes on to argue that statements of physics are a priori judgements. They classify empirical judgements (and are thus synthetic) but use concepts that are prior to experience (and are thus a priori). These concepts, or 'categories of our understanding' as Kant called them, are much like space and time in mathematics. The 'categories' are the essential framework of our knowledge. They consist of such things as quality, quantity, relation (including causality) and modality (such as existence or nonexistence). They are not part of our experience, yet we could not have any experience without them.

When we come to metaphysics, however, the opposite is true. Metaphysics has nothing to do with experience (as it is 'beyond physics'). This means we cannot apply 'categories' such as quantity and quality to metaphysics, because these are the framework of our knowledge of experience. Thus metaphysics excludes itself from the realm of synthetic a priori judgements and has no scientific basis. So if we take a metaphysical concept, such as God, we cannot make any scientific (or verifiable) statement about him, because any categories we might apply are relevant only to experience. Thus to talk of the existence (or nonexistence) of God is to misapply the categories.

In this way Kant dismissed metaphysics. Yet in doing so he built up his own alternative metaphysical system. The way Kant saw them, the 'forms of our understanding' (space and time), as well as the 'categories of our understanding' (including existence, necessity and so on), are undeniably metaphysical. We may consider space and existence to be 'out there' in the physics of our experience, but Kant did not. So his argument against metaphysics applies equally to them. We can make no synthetic a priori statements about them. They are not scientific, they are not analytic, and they are not logically necessary: they are metaphysical. And if, on the other hand, they are 'out there' in our experience, they certainly cannot be a priori concepts of our understanding.

Kant's *Critique of Practical Reason* attempts to apply a very similar system to ethics. Instead of asking if there are such things as synthetic a priori judgements, he asks if there are rules which a priori govern our will and can thus claim to be universal. Instead of the categories, he comes up with a 'categorical imperative' – which is not a part of actual moral experience but the a priori framework necessary for it. This categorical imperative he expresses as follows: 'Act only in accord with a principle which you would at the same time will to be a universal law.' Like the categories, this imperative is purely formal. The categories have no empirical content, the categorical imperative has no moral content. This categorical imperative may appear all very well, but it is wide enough to encompass the contradictory moralities of the sado-masochist as well as the peace-and-love hippie. It is also strictly rational and implies that we should regard all human beings as temperamentally identical to ourselves. But our psychology is not strictly rational, and we do not regard others as being temperamentally identical to ourselves. Nor do we wish them to be – unless we happen to be a dictator. How can we even apply such an imperative if we don't think like this or behave like this? We may subscribe to certain universal principles, but these don't cover all our moral actions. There are certain less fundamental principles which we would have no wish to apply to the moral actions of all peoples. I may abstain from cannibalism and at the same time wish to see the principle 'Eating people is wrong' universally applied. But if I abstain from murder, this does not mean that I wish a policeman to abstain from murdering a murderous hostage-taker.

It is possible to argue that such strictures do not apply, as the categorical imperative is merely the framework of morality. By our moral actions we merely imply universal principles. But such retreat into formality renders the categorical imperative itself utterly vacuous. It plainly states that we should behave in such a way that we wish all other people to behave.

FROM KANT'S WRITINGS

The following excerpt is from the opening of the Critique of Pure Reason, *where Kant prepares to lay the foundations of his philosophy. As can be seen from the second sentence, Kant begins as he means to go on. Persevere beyond this easily spotted ambush and you will soon become aware of a quality of mind that nimbly transcends the quagmire of its conveyance:*

It is beyond a doubt that all our knowledge begins with experience. For by what should our faculties be roused to act, if not by objects that affect our senses, and thus partly of themselves produce impressions, partly, again, bring the understanding itself into movement, in order to compare these, to join or disjoin them, and in this manner work up such crude material of the intimations of sense into a cognition or recognition of objects which is named experience. So far as time is concerned, then, no cognition of ours precedes experience, and with experience all our knowledge begins.

Kant goes on to argue:

Though all our knowledge begins *with* experience, it does not follow that therefore it all derives *from* experience. For it is just possible that experience is itself a compound. It is just possible, that is, that there is experience besides what is due to the impression of sense, something in addition that comes from our faculties themselves (when merely acting because of impression); and in that case, it would take long practice, it may be, to enable us to distinguish the latter, and separate it from the former.

He then asks:

Can there really be such component part of knowledge as is independent of experience, and indeed, of any impression of sense whatever? Such component part of knowledge, did it exist, was alone to be termed truly a priori; and it would evidently stand in contradistinction to what other component part of knowledge is called empirical: the latter, namely, having its source only a posteriori, or in experience.

Kant now goes further into the notion of a priori:

The expression a priori at the same time is not precise enough to designate the entire sense of the preceding question. For of many a mere empirical fact, we say that we know it a priori, simply because we do not derive it directly from experience, but from a general rule; and this, even notwithstanding that the rule itself may be so derived. For example, we say of a man that shall have undermined his house, he might have known a priori that it would fall in; he had no occasion to wait for the experience of the actual event. Nevertheless, he could not have known this absolutely a priori. For that bodies are heavy and, consequently, fall when their supports are withdrawn, this, at least, he must have known by experience beforehand.

In what follows, therefore, we shall understand by cognitions a priori, not such as are independent of this or that experience, but such as are totally independent of any experience whatsoever. Opposed to these are empirical cognitions, or such as are only possible a posteriori, or from experience. Pure, again, are those a priori cognitions which are quite free from all and every empirical admixture. Thus, for example, the proposition that all change has its cause, is an a priori proposition; but it is not, at the same time, *purely* such, for change is an idea which can only be derived from experience.

All the above quotes from *Critique of Pure Reason*, 2nd Edition (1787), Introduction, Part 1

The argument continues, and the plot thickens. This extremely rare opportunity to accompany one of the finest intellects in history as it proceeds on its original way should not be missed. To aspire to attain such heights easily defeats the entire purpose of the exercise:

What is wanted here is a criterion, by means of which we may, with certainty, distinguish what is pure from what is empirical. Now experience informs us that something *is* so and so, but not that it cannot be otherwise. *Firstly*, then, should there be a proposition such that it is thought together with its necessity, then it is a judgement a priori; and, if underived from any other, absolutely a priori. *Secondly*, experience extends to its judgements never strict or true, but only (through induction) assumptive or comparative universality; so that, properly, it can only be said: So far as we are yet aware, there is no exception to this or that rule. Should any judgement, then, be thought in strict universality, or so, that is, that exceptions are impossible, we may be sure that that judgement is no derivative from experience, but directly a priori. Empirical universality, therefore, is only an arbitrary raising of validity from that which obtains in most cases to that which holds good in all, as in the proposition, for example, that all bodies are heavy. Whereas, when strict universality attaches to a judgement, such universality points to a special cognitive source, namely, to a faculty of cognition a priori. Necessity and strict universality, therefore, are sure criteria of a priori cognition, and inseparably found together. In practice, however, as it is easier, now to apply the one and now the other, it will be advisable to avail ourselves, as occasion may suggest, of either criterion separately; for, even separately, either of them is quite infallible.

He continues with a bravura display of German metaphysical argument. Like any good medicine, this should be taken slowly, and repeatedly – only then do its efficacious qualities begin to emerge:

Now, it is easy to show that there actually are in our knowledge such necessary and, in the strictest sense, universal (consequently pure a priori) judgements. Would we have an example from science, we have only to turn to any proposition in mathematics; while, as for the most ordinary common sense, there is obviously to hand, by way of instance, the proposition that every change must have a cause, where the very notion cause so manifestly implies necessity (of connection with an effect) and strict universality (of rule), that it would be altogether lost did we derive it, like Hume, from our conjoining what simply follows with what simply precedes, through the mere habit of experience, and the consequent simple custom of connecting ideas (where the necessity could only be subjective). Besides demonstrating the actual existence in our knowledge of principles a priori by a reference to fact, we might even a priori prove as much. We might demonstrate, that is, the indispensable necessity of such principles to the very possibility of experience. For how should there be any certainty in experience, were all the rules in it only empirical and (consequently) contingent? It was hardly possible, evidently, to allow any such rules the name of first principles. But it may suffice here to have demonstrated the fact of the possession of pure cognition on our part, together with the signs of the latter. Nay, not merely judgements, but even certain ideas, may claim for themselves an a priori origin. Suppose, in the case of our empirical idea of a *body*, we successively withdraw all its empirical constituents, such as colour, consistency, weight, even impenetrability, we shall still find it impossible to withdraw the space it occupied. This space will still remain when the body itself has disappeared. In like manner, if, in regard to our empirical idea of an object in general, whether corporeal or incorporeal, we withdraw all properties known to us from experience, we shall still be unable to withdraw from it those by which we think it as substance, or as attributive to substance (though this notion of substance has more determination in it than that of an object in general). We must, therefore, overborne by the necessity with which said notion forces itself upon us, admit that it has its seat a priori in our faculties of cognition.

above quotes from *Critique of Pure Reason*, 2nd Edition (1787), Introduction, Part 2

Here Kant explains the notion of time according to his philosophy:

Time has no objective reality; it is not an accident, not a substance, and not a relation: it is a purely subjective condition, necessary because of the nature of the human mind, which co-ordinates all our sensibilities by a certain law, and is a pure intuition. We co-ordinate substances and accidents alike, according to simultaneity and succession, only through the concept of time.

Collected Works, Vol 2

Here Kant differentiates between different kinds of happiness. This comes from his essay On the Beautiful and the Sublime:

Because someone is only happy in so far as he gratifies a desire, the feeling that causes him to enjoy such great pleasures, without him needing great ability in order to do so, is certainly no trivial matter. Fat people, whose favourite artists are their cooks and whose masterpieces lie in their cellar, enjoy their common obscenities and vulgar witticisms just as much as nobler souls enjoy their more refined pursuits. An indolent fellow who loves to have books read aloud to him because he enjoys falling asleep in this fashion, the businessman who considers all pleasure a distraction apart from working out his profits on a smart business deal, someone who loves the opposite sex for the sheer pleasure of it and nothing else, the keen hunter whether he merely hunts flies like the Roman Emperor Domitian or ferocious beasts like A – all these have feelings which make them capable of experiencing pleasure in their own way, without them being envious of others or even being capable of conceiving of other pleasures. This kind of feeling, which can take place without any thought at all, I shall completely disregard ...

Fine feeling, which I shall now consider, is for the most part of two kinds: the feeling of the sublime and that of the beautiful. Each gives us pleasure, but in different ways. The sight of a snowcapped mountain peak rising above the clouds, the description of a wild storm, or Milton's depiction of the kingdom of hell – each of these gives us joy, but mingled with terror. On the other hand, the sight of flower-covered meadows, valleys with winding streams and grazing flocks, the description of Elysium, or Homer's depiction of the girdle of Venus, these also give us a pleasant sensation, but one that is joyful and happy. In order to feel the former sensation we must have a *feeling of the sublime*, but in order to experience the latter properly we must have a *feeling of the beautiful*.

On the Beautiful and the Sublime, Sec 1

A rare example of Kantian poetry. This was written in 1782 on the occasion of the death of Pastor Lilienthal, who had married Kant's parents:

Was auf das Leben folgt deckt tiefe Finsterniss;
Was uns zu thun gebuhrt, dess sind wis nur gewiss.

(What comes after life is hidden in deep darkness;
What we are expected to do, that alone we know.)

An even rarer example, this time of Kantian humour, a somewhat desiccated and elusive quality. This comes from the opening of his essay 'Perpetual Peace':

PERPETUAL PEACE

Whether this satirical inscription on a Dutch innkeeper's sign, upon which a churchyard was painted, has for its object mankind in general, or in particular the governors of states, who are insatiable of war; or whether it points merely towards those philosophers who indulge the sweet dream of a perpetual peace, it is impossible to decide . . .

The following goes a long way towards explaining the popularity of Kant's geography lectures with the citizens of Königsberg. It was written by Dr J.H. Stirling, a nineteenth-century British member of the Philosophical Society of Berlin.

[In Kant's geography lectures] he cannot help referring to some of the most interesting facts that have reached him . . . Negroes are born white, all to a ring around the navel. The ibis dies the moment it quits Egypt. The lion is so noble, he will not put a paw upon a woman . . . If you make a cup of the rhinoceros's horn, any poison will splinter it . . . There is a mussel in Italy that gives out so much light that you can read by it. In Languedoc there is a hot spring that hatches eggs ... Wild beasts eat only Negroes in Gambia, and leave Europeans alone. The Negroes in America are immensely fond of dog's flesh, and all the dogs bark at them.

According to Dr Stirling, these views were 'all gravely propounded'.

CHRONOLOGY OF SIGNIFICANT PHILOSOPHICAL DATES

6th C BC	The beginning of Western philosophy with Thales of Miletus.
End of 6th C BC	Death of Pythagoras.
399 BC	Socrates sentenced to death in Athens.
c 387 BC	Plato founds the Academy in Athens, the first university.
335 BC	Aristotle founds the Lyceum in Athens, a rival school to the Academy.
AD 324	Emperor Constantine moves capital of Roman Empire to Byzantium.
AD 400	St Augustine writes his *Confessions*. Philosophy absorbed into Christian theology.
AD 410	Sack of Rome by Visigoths heralds opening of Dark Ages.
AD 529	Closure of Academy in Athens by Emperor Justinian marks end of Hellenic thought.
Mid-13th C	Thomas Aquinas writes his commentaries on Aristotle. Era of Scholasticism.

CHRONOLOGY OF KANT'S LIFE

22 April 1724	Immanuel Kant born in Königsberg in East Prussia.
1737	Kant's mother dies.
1741	Kant enters the University of Königsberg.
1746	Kant's father dies and he is forced to leave the university to support himself as a private tutor.
1755	He finally takes his degree at the University of Königsberg.
1755	Becomes *privatdozent* (equivalent of junior lecturer) at the university and delivers lectures on mathematics, philosophy, anthropology and physical geography.
1770	Appointed professor of logic and metaphysics.
1781	Publishes *Critique of Pure Reason*.
1788	Publishes *Critique of Practical Reason*.
1790	Publishes *Critique of Judgement*.
October 1803	Falls ill for the first time in his life.

| 12 February 1804 | Dies and is buried in Königsberg Cathedral. |

CHRONOLOGY OF KANT'S ERA

1739	The Scottish philosopher David Hume publishes *A Treatise of Human Nature*.
1743	Birth of Thomas Jefferson.
1750–1752	Voltaire takes up residence at the court of Frederick II of Prussia in Potsdam.
1751	Death of French philosopher La Mettrie.
1759	Founding of British Museum.
1762	Rousseau publishes *Émile*, which causes Kant to break his routine and miss his afternoon walk.
1770	Birth of Hegel.
1774	Goethe publishes *The Sorrows of Young Werther*.
1776	American Declaration of Independence. Death of Hume.
1778	Death of Rousseau.
1789	French Revolution. George Washington becomes first president of the United States.
1799	Napoleon becomes first consul of France.
1804	Napoleon becomes ruler of Germany.

RECOMMENDED READING

David Appelbaum, *The Vision of Kant* (Element Books, 1995).

Michael Friedman, *Kant and the Exact Sciences* (Harvard University Press, 1992).

Paul Guyer, ed., *The Cambridge Companion to Kant* (Cambridge University Press, 1992).

Ben-Ami Scharfstein, *The Philosophers: Their Lives and the Nature of Their Thought* (Oxford University Press, 1989).

Norman K. Smith, ed., *Critique of Pure Reason* (St Martin's, 1969).

INDEX

A NOTE ON THE AUTHOR

PAUL STRATHERN was educated at Trinity College, Dublin, and lectures in mathematics and philosophy at Kingston University. He has written five novels, one of which won a Somerset Maugham Prize. His most recent works include *Dr Strangelove's Game: A Brief History of Economic Genius* and *Mendeleyev's Dream: The Quest for the Elements*, which was shortlisted for the Aventis Science Prize. He has also written for many journals including the *Observer* (London), *Wall Street Journal* and *New Scientist*. His popular Philosophers in 90 Minutes series is being published worldwide in fifteen languages.